Original title:
Sprouting Stories

Copyright © 2025 Creative Arts Management OÜ
All rights reserved.

Author: Atticus Thornton
ISBN HARDBACK: 978-1-80566-665-3
ISBN PAPERBACK: 978-1-80566-950-0

In the Heart of the Green

In the garden, a gnome starts to dance,
Chasing butterflies without a chance.
Worms in a conga line groove and sway,
While daisies giggle, they join the play.

A cabbage plots its mischievous schemes,
With radishes whispering silly dreams.
Tomatoes wear hats, quite proud and round,
In this hilarity that's garden-bound.

Foliage Fantasies

In a forest where squirrels wear ties,
And mushrooms sing with delighted cries.
The oak tree plays hide and seek with the pines,
While dandelions dance in decent lines.

A beetle brings cupcakes to the affair,
And snails leave trails of glittering flair.
The wind stirs laughter through every leaf,
As laughter echoes beyond disbelief.

Interwoven Dreams

Bamboo sticks poke each other's sides,
As crickets give commands to dance with pride.
Vines twirl like ribbons in an endless song,
While the sun beams down—what could go wrong?

A group of flowers start a trivia game,
The daisies claim they invented fame.
Sunflowers wear shades, declaring a trend,
In this wacky world where fun won't end.

Mythos of the Meadow

In a meadow where clouds wear silly hats,
Bouncing bunnies have epic chats.
Chickens juggle eggs while chewing gum,
As flowers nod along to their fun drum.

The grass holds meetings for all to join,
Debating which insect is the most fine.
With each blooming joke, they brighten the day,
In this light-hearted realm where giggles play.

Leaves of Legacy

Once a tiny seed, full of dreams,
Beneath the soil, it quietly schemes.
A leaf pops out, oh what a sight,
Waving around, with all its might.

In the wind, it plays a game,
Telling tales of nature's fame.
A daisy chases, a butterfly flies,
While roots make jokes in disguise.

A Tapestry of Tendrils

Vines intertwine, a messy affair,
Whispering secrets without a care.
They tickle the fence and wiggle in glee,
Binding their stories, just wait and see.

With a twist and a turn, they plot and plan,
Imagining worlds, how funny they can!
In every curl, a prank awaits,
Fun-loving tendrils, the jesters of states.

The Chronicle of Growth

A sprout wakes up, yawning wide,
In the sun's embrace, it takes pride.
Each inch it stretches, each leaf unfurls,
Claiming its space in the world that swirls.

"Oh look at me!" it giggles and beams,
Dancing with the breeze, chasing dreams.
A caterpillar joins, they waltz around,
Sharing laughter in the vibrant ground.

Fern Fragments

Ferns unfurl their fronds with flair,
Dancing like they just don't care.
With every flick, they share a jest,
   Telling tales of nature's best.

"Look at us," they quip with glee,
"Masters of shade, wild and free!"
In the forest's dim, they jump and play,
Cheerful comrades, brightening the day.

Unexpected Blossoms

In a garden filled with socks,
Grew flowers made of rocks.
They giggled as they bloomed,
In colors bright and loomed.

A bee once tried to buzz,
But tripped on all the fuzz.
It laughed and spun around,
Socks dancing on the ground.

Rivers of Renewal

A river flowed with lemonade,
Where ducks wore shades and played.
They paddled on a raft,
With squeals of silly craft.

Fish wore tiny party hats,
Sipping tea with playful chats.
They splashed and made a mess,
In a world of happiness.

Unwritten Blossoms

Once a pen sat on a tree,
Wishing it could write with glee.
A squirrel took it for a spin,
And wrote a tale by accident.

Words flew out like butterflies,
Painting dreams across the skies.
Each letter danced and twirled,
Creating a whole new world.

Stories in the Sunlight

In sunlight's warmth, stories gleamed,
A bench of whispers, how it seemed.
A cat told tales of mice in shoes,
While kids laughed at the silly news.

A sunbeam spun a yarn so bright,
Of clouds that danced in pure delight.
And shadows joined the fray with glee,
Creating laughter, wild and free.

The Roots of Tomorrow

In a garden of dreams so wide,
Little roots play peek-a-boo, they hide.
One claimed it was a race to grow,
But tripped on a worm, oh no, oh no!

They giggle and wiggle, twist and twirl,
Determined to show off their leafy swirl.
With a dash of dirt and a sprinkle of sun,
They plot their adventures, oh what fun!

Petals of Promise

Petals whisper secrets loud,
About a bee who's far too proud.
He bragged he'd win the flower crown,
But tripped on pollen, fell right down!

They chuckle as they dance in breeze,
Sharing jokes with the buzzing bees.
With colors bright and laughter shared,
Each petal knows how much they dared!

Unfolding Chapters

In books of blooms, the pages turn,
A sunflower winks, it's his turn to learn.
He read about growing oh so tall,
But got stuck in a pickle, rolled like a ball!

The daisies laughed, they roared with glee,
As the sunflower tried to climb a tree.
Each chapter's full of silly strife,
Yet in their heart, they cherish life!

Echoes of the Earth

From below, the soil giggles wide,
As worms squirm and give it a ride.
One said, 'I've got a tale to share,'
About a plant who lost its hair!

The rocks chimed in with laughs and cheer,
'Oh, that green guy had quite a fear!'
With echoes of joy, they spin their yarns,
In the cradle of nature, where laughter adorns.

The Storytime of the Seasons

Winter whispers in frost's embrace,
Snowflakes giggle, at nature's pace.
Spring brings tulips, with cheerful cheer,
Squirrels wear boots for the coming year.

Summer's sun rays dance on the grass,
Children chase shadows, oh how they pass!
Autumn drops leaves like confetti flies,
Pumpkins parade in whimsical guise.

Fragments of Life's Green Tapestry

Dandelions in a race, oh so spry,
Wishing for wings, to learn how to fly.
Ladybugs gossip on leaves so bright,
Ants have a party to celebrate night.

Frogs in a band, with their ribbiting sound,
Croaking in tune, they hop all around.
Mice wear tuxedos, oh what a sight,
Dancing with moonbeams till morning light.

Radiant Reckonings from the Ground Up

Through the soil, the roots start to tickle,
Earthworms giggle, in mud they wiggle.
Sprouts have secrets, they promise to tell,
Of ladybug tales, oh what a swell!

Caterpillars in line, a curious queue,
Dreaming of wings, to paint skies anew.
Sunflowers fuss, competing for space,
While bees wear tiny hats, in their race.

Nature's Pen: Writing in Blossoms

Blossoms write letters on petals so soft,
Comets of pollen that dance and loft.
Trees tell tales with their rustling leaves,
Whispering giggles, teasing the eaves.

The rain drops like ink, in puddles they'll play,
Drawing funny faces that wash away.
Clouds become artists, crafting shapes on high,
Painting the story of sun in the sky.

Branches of Imagination

In a tree where ideas grow,
Squirrels argue, steal the show.
Each branch holds a tale untold,
Of acorns dreaming, brave and bold.

A bird dips low, a joke it sings,
While ants conspire in tiny rings.
Beneath the shade, laughter unfolds,
As whispers of wisdom brightly mold.

Clouds drift by, they're part of the game,
Mistaken for sheep, they're not quite the same.
Each raindrop giggles, splashing down,
As puddles form a laughter crown.

In this realm where fancies play,
Imagination grows day by day.
Twisty trunks and tangled vines,
All tell tales of funny lines.

The Story of Each Leaf

Once a bud on the branch so spry,
A leaf peeked out to wave goodbye.
It slipped and slid in a breezy dance,
Chasing shadows, in a leaf's mischance.

Whispers floated from tree to tree,
As leaves debated their own decree.
"I'm the best green, can't you see?"
With friendly banter, they all agree!

A gust of wind swept through the park,
Sending leaves spiraling, like a lark.
They tumbled down with a shimmering cheer,
Landing on noses, giggling in fear.

As summer fades, they change their tune,
Autumn jokes with a colorful swoon.
With laughter echoed in every rustle,
Each leaf holds a story, a leafy tussle.

Flourishing Voices

In a meadow where daisies sing,
Petals gossip about the spring.
Bees buzz in with a silly grin,
Spreading tales thick as honey can spin.

The grass hums softly, a tickle of breeze,
While frogs croak loudly, hoping to please.
They hold a contest, who's loudest of all?
With croaks and chirps, they have a ball!

Sunflowers stand, tall and proud,
With heads held high, they shout aloud.
"We're the tallest, we rule the sky!"
While critters giggle, oh me, oh my!

Yet as daylight starts to wane,
Crickets strum a serenade in vain.
Their nightly symphony plays with delight,
In this whimsical world, all feels right.

The Narrative of Nature

Beneath the bark, the stories swell,
Nature whispers its funny spell.
From the roots deep down, to the sky so blue,
Every creature has a tale or two.

A turtle dreamed it could fly like a bird,
While a snail snickered, "Well, that's absurd!"
In the mud, frogs held a grand debate,
About the silliest way to navigate.

The sun chuckled, casting shadows long,
While flowers swayed to nature's song.
Each rustle of leaves, a punchline awaits,
As critters gather for comedic debates.

Nature's laughter, wild and bright,
In every corner, joy takes flight.
From tiny seeds to the towering trees,
Life's funny tales float on the breeze.

Fragments of Flora

In the garden, odd plants grow,
Whispering secrets, to and fro.
Daisies wearing hats of green,
Murmuring dreams, quite unseen.

An onion danced, oh what a sight,
In moonlit glow, it took to flight.
Garlic giggled, in a wink,
Said, "Let's party, don't you think?"

Frolicking petals, a wiggly vine,
Serenading bees with sweetened wine.
Tulips in tutus, doing a jig,
Even the grasses join in, so big!

Fragrant blooms in silly attire,
Turning the plot into a choir.
Laughter blooms where veggies roam,
In this garden, all's a home!

Whims of the Wilderness

In the woods, a squirrel pranced,
Doing the tango, all quite enhanced.
A chipmunk wore sparkling shoes,
Finding treasure, not to lose.

Trees told tales with creaky laughter,
A deer played tag, what a disaster!
Bushes chuckled, swaying wide,
As the fox attempted to glide.

Rabbits rehearsed for a play,
Critters all in a cabaret.
A wise owl hooted some advice,
"Join the fun, don't be precise!"

In this wild, bizarre ballet,
Nature's quirks come out to play.
With every rustle, giggles bloom,
Whims of wilderness, a funny room!

Legends of the Lush

In a patch of green so grand and wide,
Grew a legend only cats abide.
They'd gather 'round a garden gnome,
And plot adventures, far from home.

But one brave fern turned up its frond,
Claiming it knew of a treasure beyond.
A missing sock or a lost cat paw,
The tales grew grand, with much guffaw.

Caterpillars hosted a grand feast,
While ladybugs danced, never ceased.
Hilarious myths of the blooming ground,
In the lush, the funny's always found!

Legends unfold 'neath the shimmering sun,
Where each leaf's whisper is endless fun.
Folks may doubt, but who would disprove,
The antics of nature's eternal groove?

The Garden's Tales

In the garden, gossip flows,
Petunia fumbles, and everyone knows.
With tiny tales, they spin and twirl,
Each flower's secret gives a whirl.

The marigolds share jokes so bright,
While roses quip and tickle the night.
A snail is known as the speedy chap,
He swears he once took a long, fast nap.

A cucumber wore shades, feeling quite suave,
While carrots burst out with a low, deep laugh.
Sunflowers cheer in their tall embrace,
Tickling the daisies, a playful race!

The garden's lore, a riotous spree,
Where every plant has a joke for thee.
Join in the fun, in this plot so bright,
Tales of the garden give pure delight!

The Voice of the Vines

In a garden full of chatter,
The tomatoes start their gossip,
They share tales of the fertilizer,
Hoping to grow a bit taller.

The cucumbers wear bright hats,
While carrots sport a fancy tie,
They argue who's the best at jokes,
But laughs just make the rabbits fly.

The radishes blush in silence,
While peas get tangled in their games,
They dream of running marathons,
But they can't outrun their own names.

When dusk arrives, the cabbage creaks,
Telling secrets to the moon,
The plants laugh as night ensues,
Sharing dreams of jazz and tunes.

Echoes of Ecosystems

The ants march in perfect lines,
Discussing breadcrumbs, small and round,
With plans of feasts, they plot routines,
While snails move slow with purpose found.

The frogs croak jokes by the pond,
While turtles ponder on their speed,
"Why hurry?" says the wise old frog,
"Life's a race, but don't you breed!"

Bees buzz tales of sweet success,
As they dance from bloom to bloom,
In nature's halls of funny flings,
Where pollen's spread, there's lots of room.

If trees could laugh, they'd shake their leaves,
At squirrels who steal their snacks with glee,
Echoing giggles through branches high,
Nature's playground, wild and free.

Nature's Narrative

In the forest, leaves tell tales,
Of critters bold, and silly falls,
Squirrels slip from branches thick,
While owls hoot out their silly calls.

A fox prances with fancy flair,
Strutting pride, like a runway star,
His whiskers twitch, a cheeky grin,
He thinks he's quite the best by far.

The flowers gossip, soft and sweet,
About the bees who always tease,
"Catch us if you can!" they sing,
As petals flutter in the breeze.

When sunsets paint the skies with gold,
Creatures share their world-renowned game,
For every laugh under the stars,
Nature's joy is never the same.

Reveries of Rebirth

A seed once dreamed of sunny skies,
And sprouted up with funny doubts,
"Do I have leaves? Will I find friends?"
And hope the nature all shouts out.

In springtime's laugh, the daisies bloom,
With petals bright, they wave hello,
While dandelions kick up dust,
In the wind, their wishes flow.

The worms below have funny talks,
About the dirt and what's for lunch,
"I found a boot, how bold!" they cheer,
With foggy glooms, they throw a punch.

As time moves on, life turns and spins,
New stories weave through roots and vines,
In each rebirth, a chuckle waits,
Nature's tale in jester's lines.

Greenhouse of Ideas

In a glass house where thoughts collide,
Laughter blooms like flowers wide.
Plants whisper jokes, oh what a sight,
Growing punchlines under sunlight.

Tomatoes gossip, green beans tease,
Witty banter rustles in the breeze.
Cucumber laughs, it's quite the show,
In this garden where ideas grow.

Funny roots sneak beneath the ground,
Tickling soil with laughter sound.
Petals dance to a rhythm new,
Sprouting humor, in every hue.

Fertilizer's got tales to tell,
Of plants that grow in a wishing well.
Each vine a story, wild and free,
In this greenhouse, joy's the key.

Dreams in the Dirt

Beneath the surface, secrets lie,
With worms who laugh and squirrels who sigh.
Grains of soil chat, sharing dreams,
In a world where nothing's as it seems.

Seeds tell stories of countries vast,
Of sunlit days and shadows cast.
Potatoes don hats, oh what a fuss,
While carrots giggle in a leafy bus!

The earth is alive with tales old and new,
As daisies debate their favorite hue.
With roots entwined, they joke and play,
In this muddy realm, they savor each day.

Dreams sprout up with a quirky twist,
In this garden, nothing's amiss.
From weeds to blooms, all have a say,
In the dirt that holds them, they laugh away.

The Song of the Saplings

Saplings sway with a rhythm fine,
Singing tunes of a plant-based rhyme.
Branching out with every note,
In this green choir, joy's remote.

Chirping leaves, a wind-sent laugh,
Woodpecker knocking, a quirky staff.
Each sprout a solo, a dance divine,
Tiny ticket to the leafy line.

They harmonize with the bouncing bees,
Tickling the hearts of all who seize.
In their world, each giggle's clear,
As petals chime, they hold so dear.

Frolicking foliage, jump and sway,
In this melody, they find their way.
Nature's concert, full of cheer,
A song of saplings, loud and clear.

The Language of Leaves

Leaves conspire in the morning light,
Speaking secrets with sheer delight.
In rustling whispers, they plot and plan,
A leafy comedy that's grand!

Oak tells tales of the squirrels' pranks,
Maple chimes in with syrupy thanks.
Pine needles giggle in the breeze,
Sharing mishaps of wandering bees.

Golden rays catch the laughter shared,
In the forest, each moment's bared.
Leaves wave flags of their funny esteem,
In this foliage feast, we dream.

Words in the wind dance and sway,
Teaching us to laugh every day.
In the chorus of greenery, we believe,
There's magic alive in the language of leaves.

Nature's Unwritten Memoirs

In the forest, trees confide,
Tales of dance from roots to sky.
Little squirrels steal the show,
While mushrooms giggle, soft and low.

The wind writes notes upon the leaves,
Each rustle whispers, 'What a tease!'
Frogs in tuxedos croak a tune,
As butterflies waltz with the moon.

A deer in stripes, quite the sight,
Claims it's fashion week tonight.
With acorns like hats, the critters cheer,
'Nature's runway is finally here!'

Beneath the stars, they gather round,
Echoes of laughter fill the ground.
In the wild, stories weave and spin,
Where every creature has a grin.

Hushed Whispers Beneath the Canopy

Leaves gossip as the breezes tease,
Who wore what at last night's breeze?
The owls exchange their nightly jokes,
While raccoons plan their heist for folks.

Mushrooms sit in circles tight,
Exchanging secrets, holding tight.
'That snail had quite the funny tale,'
'His slow race was a total fail!'

The spiders weave their gossip webs,
Chatting 'bout the best of ebbs.
With each dew drop, a secret shared,
The forest floor is fully prepared.

Beneath the boughs, jesters abound,
Where every chuckle wraps around.
In the green of night, stories twine,
With whispers sweet and just divine.

The Art of Growing Wisdom

In the garden, giggles sprout,
As daisies talk of what they're about.
The carrots boast of lengths so grand,
While lettuce chats of the cool, damp land.

Each seed a dream, just waiting for light,
Planning their parties, oh what a sight!
Tomato plants wearing ruby crowns,
Claiming to be the toast of town!

The radishes whisper of spicy fame,
'We've got the zest, don't care for the game!'
As sunflower heads nod and sway,
In leafy laughter, they dance and play.

Butterflies flutter, spreading delight,
'Pollinate dreams with all your might!'
In this patch of colors and fun,
Wisdom blossoms, one by one.

Bursting Forth With Life's Lessons

A tiny seed with dreams so grand,
Wonders how to make a stand.
With sun as a guide and rain as a friend,
It stretches out, the sky to blend.

The blooms erupt in shades so bright,
Teaching the bees to dance with delight.
In petals soft, sweet scent is found,
The buzz of life, a joyful sound.

Squirrels take notes on acorn trends,
While chipmunks debate on cheese for friends.
Nature's classroom, a lively spree,
Lessons learned with glee, carefree.

In every sprout, a yarn unfurls,
Each tale's a giggle, each twist twirls.
Bursting forth, with laughter's grace,
Life's little quirks, we heartily embrace.

Seeds of Tomorrow's Echoes

In the garden of dreams, seeds take flight,
With tiny ambitions, they reach for the light.
Each one a story, in soil they conspire,
To sprout funny tales, as they climb ever higher.

Worms gather round, like an audience keen,
Cheering for antics that only they've seen.
A potato jokes, "I'm the root of the fun!"
While carrots keep tumbling, catching the sun.

Bees hum a tune, a delightful refrain,
Tickling the leaves with a whimsical strain.
They dance 'round the daisies, all dressed up in cheer,
No summer day grumpy, not even a sneer.

So here's to the seeds, in their quirky quest,
Growing tales of humor, we like them the best!
With laughter in petals, and joy in the roots,
Nature's own jesters, in their green, leafy suits.

Blooming Narratives

Petals burst forth with a giggle and glee,
As buds share secrets with each buzzing bee.
In a patch of sunflowers, they tell silly tales,
Of how they once traveled on wind-swept gales.

The tulips gossip, their heads held up high,
"You won't believe what I heard from the sky!"
Daisies all chuckle, they play peek-a-boo,
While violets brag, "We're cooler than you!"

In every bright petal, lies a laugh or a rhyme,
Nature's own jesters, freezing time.
Through sweet scented breezes and mirthful prance,
These blooms weave laughter in a flowery dance.

So let's celebrate blooms, and their playful jest,
Crafting narratives funny, we think they're the best!
With each gentle breeze, a new tale will arise,
In the garden of whimsy beneath sunny skies.

The Language of New Beginnings

In the dawn of the sprouts, where laughter is sown,
Little green whispers make their jokes known.
A cucumber quips, "I'm on a roll!"
While turnips play tag, digging down in a hole.

As raindrops come falling like giggles from clouds,
Seeds of humor sprout under laughter's loud shrouds.
The sun beams a smile, brightening the plot,
While the carrots compete for the funniest spot.

Each leaf speaks a language, both silly and sweet,
With roots in the soil, where laughter and play meet.
A chorus of colors, a riot of cheer,
Telling us stories we can all hear!

So let's revel in nurture, and joyfully grow,
In the language of laughter, there's always a show!
With chatter of blooms, and whispers of greens,
A fest of beginnings where humor convenes.

Chronicles of Nature's Revival

In a world of green chaos, where stories unfold,
All creatures unite, both daring and bold.
The squirrels have meetings to share all their schemes,
While flowers plot pranks in their colorful dreams.

The frogs wear their crowns, reigning over the bog,
Croaking in rhythm, a ribbiting slog.
The butterflies flit, adorned in their best,
As they giggle at petals that bloomed with great zest.

The sun shines its rays, a spotlight of fun,
While daisies compete for the title of "Sun!"
Amidst all this laughter, the world feels so free,
In chronicles funny, where all can agree.

So come witness the tales, in gardens where mirth,
Tells us of joy in the soil of the earth!
With a wink and a nod to the life that we share,
Nature's revival brings laughter everywhere.

Verdant Vignettes

In a garden where veggies play,
A carrot told a beet 'Hey,
I tried to grow a mustache,
But I just ended in the trash.'

The radish danced in a funky dress,
Said, 'Who knew I'd be such a mess?
My leaves are wild, my roots are shy,
But watch me twirl as I say goodbye!'

The peas in pods were holding court,
Plotting schemes of veggie sport,
They laughed and joked, had tons of fun,
A salad league was just begun!

In the soil, a tale began,
Of secrets shared by plant and man,
With every sprout and silly cheer,
The garden's laughter filled the year.

Life in the Seedbed

In darkened corners of the earth,
Tiny seeds plot their rebirth,
'This sprouting business,' one seed cried,
'Is nothing short of a wild ride!'

A bean pole whispered just for fun,
'Let's take bets on who'll be number one!
Will it be me with my climbing spree,
Or that tulip, sitting like a queen bee?'

The weeds chimed in with a cheeky grin,
'We may be pesky, but where's the sin?
Without a little chaos here and there,
This garden life would be quite bare!'

Each day they stretched, each day they grew,
Telling jokes like only seeds do,
In the seedbed of dreams, under the sun,
Life is funny, and so much fun!

The Language of Flora

In the flower patch, blooms shared some tea,
A daisy said, 'Just look at me!
I'm twirling so bright, like a dance of delight,
While that tall sunflower looks a bit contrite!'

'Fear not!' said a petal, full of cheer,
'Your giant friend just needs a beer,
He's been standing straight in the sun too long,
Let's sing him a song, wouldn't that be wrong?'

The violets giggled in hues of blue,
'Imagine if we just grew like you!
With mustaches and capes, what a scene,
We'd be the boldest blooms ever seen!'

So they fluttered and feasted in light's embrace,
Shaping tales with beauty and grace,
In the language of flowers, fun filled the air,
With laughter and joy beyond compare!

Chronicles of Reclamation

In an abandoned lot, where weeds took flight,
A dandelion stood, 'I'm ready to fight!
Let's turn this rubble to a grand parade,
With colors and blooms, let's not be afraid!'

A rusty can joined with a clatter and clang,
'In this garden of dreams, let's all let it hang,
We'll show the world how weeds can shine,
With a bit of sun and some funky design!'

Old tires turned to comfy seats,
While florals sprouted from concrete beats,
Together they laughed, in this reclaimed land,
Each blossom a story, perfectly planned.

Through laughter, colors, and mingling roots,
They wrote their epic in leafy suits,
In the chronicles of life, the lesson was clear,
Even in chaos, humor's always near!

Trellis of Time

In a garden of whimsy, tales intertwine,
A twist of the vine, a joke on the line.
Petunias gossip with passion and glee,
While carrots debate the best way to pee.

The sun chuckles bright, coaxing sprouts from the ground,
As rabbits munch leaves, with no care around.
The daisies are dancing, in quite the ballet,
While worms wriggle by, showing off on display.

Each petal a secret, each stem has a grin,
The wind whispers stories of where they have been.
With laughter and light, they blossom in rhyme,
Oh, what a time in the trellis of time!

So here's to the veggies, the blooms, and the lore,
To the gardening gaffes that we just can't ignore.
Let's raise a toast high, to the flora divine,
In this tale of the garden, we all intertwine.

The Unfurling Saga

From tiny acorns, a big joke's to sprout,
As oak trees giggle, their branches about.
A squirrel tells tales of a nut he once lost,
While ivy climbs high, without counting the cost.

The daisies debate who has the best bloom,
While marigolds plot to take up more room.
The sun plays a prank, casting shadows so wide,
As petals all flutter, like they're in a ride.

The roots trade old stories of storms they survived,
While vines try to sneak up, quite sure they have jived.
The bees buzz along, with laughter in flight,
As they share their sweet nectar and dance with delight.

In this unfurling saga, where fun lives and breathes,
The plants weave their tales, on the soft summer leaves.
With each gentle sway, their laughter resounds,
In the world of the greens, where joy knows no bounds.

Serenade of the Seedlings

Oh tiny seedlings, oh what a sight,
Swaying and singing from morning to night.
With roots all tangled, in a giggling race,
To see who can grow at the fastest pace!

The sun beams a wink, as they stretch for the sky,
While clouds tease the flowers, they flutter and sigh.
The beetles all boast of the tricks that they know,
And the sunflowers nod, stealing each little show.

A worm brings a tale, of a dig that went wrong,
Of how he was lost, then found where he'd belong.
The ivy shared secrets of a neighboring fence,
With laughter that lingers—and makes perfect sense.

In this serenade, each sprout takes a chance,
To twirl and to whirl in a green-loving dance.
With chortles and giggles in their garden café,
The seedlings unite, adding joy to the day.

Chronicles of Change

In the chronicles written in dirt and in dew,
Each sprout holds a story with a whimsical view.
When petals start blushing, and buds burst with cheer,
The tales whisper softly, for all plants to hear.

A pumpkin once thought he would never be round,
Grows big with surprise, rolling right on the ground.
While peas in their pods trade their secrets with pride,
Laughing at troubles that they've had to bide.

With raindrops like laughter, the leaves start to sway,
As bees tell the flowers what happened today.
The breeze plays a tune, a nature-made song,
With roots deep in stories, where all creatures belong.

So here's to the changes, the chuckles, the fun,
In gardens where laughter and life have begun.
Let's savor each moment, let our joy be the range,
In the vibrant, green world of the chronicles of change.

The Unseen Sprout

In the garden, secrets lie,
A tiny sprout gives a sly eye.
It wiggles and dances with delight,
Whispering tales of its leafy flight.

With roots that tickle and tickle more,
It giggles softly, a giggly chore.
"Oh, the things I've seen from below,
Don't ask me, I won't tell, you know!"

The worms roll their eyes, what a tease!
They chuckle in dirt, sharing the breeze.
"If sprouts could talk, what tales they'd weave!
But secrets are funny - you've got to believe!"

So, next time you see a sprout on its way,
Remember the stories it won't say.
With every inch it stretches and grows,
Lies the adventure that nobody knows.

Stories Beneath the Surface

Down in the dirt, where shadows play,
A beetle recounts its busy day.
"I met a pebble, so round and bright,
It claimed to be a star, what a sight!"

A root pipes up, feeling quite bold,
"I'm the life-source, like tales of old!
Through water and soil, I weave my thread,
There's mischief below that's never been said."

A mighty worm, with a wordy jest,
"I've traveled far, I'm quite the guest!
With stories of cabbages and game of chance,
With a wiggle and jiggle, all plants will dance!"

Every tale shared beneath the ground,
Is sprinkled with humor, cleverly found.
So if you dig deep, bring a smile,
You might hear laughter that lasts for a while.

Metamorphosis of the Meadow

Once a patch of plain old grass,
Dreamed of a life with a little sass.
It sprouted dreams of flowers and hues,
Realized its potential, wore fancy shoes!

Butterflies chuckled as they flew by,
"Look at the meadow, oh my oh my!
It's gone and flipped, what a sight to behold,
From green to glam, such stories untold!"

The daisies, giggling, quite enjoyed the game,
Deciding to change, it became a lame name.
"Call me 'Daffy,' I'll rule with flair!
Watch me twirl in the warm spring air!"

As the meadow frolicked in newfound delight,
It boasted of tales from morning till night.
With each rolling laugh, a leaf would quirk,
Turns out transformation is quite the perk!

Narrative Blooms

In a pot so cozy, tales begin,
Little petals whisper, 'Let's spin!'
Each bloom with secrets, bright and bold,
Ready to share what they've withhold.

"I once was shy, stuck in a bud,
But now I'm dazzling, bursting with 'udd!'
Listen closely, I've tales to unfold,
Of bees with costumes that brilliantly gold!"

As the sun rises, the flowers cheer,
"Look at us now, we shine with no fear!
With colors that clash and scents that sway,
Every little laugh takes drudgery away!"

So gather 'round, come see the show,
These blooms have stories, as quick as you go.
With petals that giggle and leave a mark,
Every laugh matters, even in the dark!

Growth in Quiet Corners

In the nook of a room, a plant took a stand,
Spilling secrets of soil, not meant for the hand.
It sprouted a hat from a sock on the floor,
And danced with a teacup, begging for more.

The cat eyed the leaves, as if they were prey,
While the spider spun tales of the games they'd play.
A fern told a joke that was hard to believe,
About how a cactus became an old cleave.

With whispers of growth, and a giggle or two,
The corners were full of adventures anew.
Each leaf had a laugh, with a story to share,
In this silly abode, life floated on air.

So next time you wander to a space dull and bare,
Remember the magic that's floating out there.
It's hidden, but ready to burst from its seam—
In the growth of the quiet, life knows how to dream.

Shadows of Once Upon A Time

In a garden once bloomed a rose with a grin,
It wore silly shoes, had a penchant for spin.
Tales of the past tickled leaves overhead,
As violets chattered of the stories they bred.

A gnome with a beard like a wild woolly beast,
Cooked up strange potions at his mushroom feast.
He whispered of giants who danced in the rain,
Modeling capers that were downright insane.

The daisies knew secrets, but laughed them away,
About adventures that happened in play.
Of shadows that leapt like they knew how to fly,
While the petals rolled by, wearing hats made of pie.

So gather your dreams, let your laughter unfold,
In the shadows of tales, past and new, bright and bold.
The garden will chuckle, with stories to lend,
In a whimsical world where the giggles won't end.

Budding Dreams

In the soil of a nap, where the laughter takes flight,
Dreams began with a wink, 'Let's party all night!'
Tiny seeds shared snacks, while sprouting old pranks,
Telling tales of the skies with a flurry of flanks.

A sunflower blushed, 'I'm the tallest of all!'
While daisies chimed in with a jingling call.
The beans had opinions, mostly about beans,
And how they could rule all the flower-filled scenes.

At dusk, they'd all gather for a grand game,
Of who could tell stories with the wildest name.
'Once upon a thunder,' a petal declared,
And to everyone's shock, the sky actually bared!

So next time you see, in a patch on the ground,
A hint of a dream, let the laughter abound.
For in every small sprout, there's a tale yet untold,
Waiting for giggles in the sun's warm gold.

Fables in the Foliage

In the brush of the woods, where the leaves like to chat,
Stories of squirrels and a very sly cat.
They conjured the myths of a kooky parade,
Where mushrooms wore glasses and the trees all swayed.

With vines acting goofy, and roots keen to jest,
They spoke of the critters who thought they were best.
A hedgehog in armor, a turtle in lace,
Joined forces to keep the wild weeds in place.

A butterfly flapped with such marvelous glee,
That it spun up a tale about how it could see.
Drawing lines in the air with a wiggly flair,
As the fog rolled on past, with gossip to share.

So wander through foliage, where the stories take wing,
And the laughter of nature is an outrageous thing.
For in every corner of woodlands and glens,
Lie fables and dreams where the nonsense begins.

The Flora Fable

In the garden, a pea tried to sing,
But got tangled up in a stubborn spring.
A snail danced slow, on a leaf so wide,
Claiming it was a rollercoaster ride!

A beetroot blushed, said, 'Look at me!'
While carrots giggled with such glee.
Dandelions whispered, 'We're stars, you know,'
As they waved to the bumblebees below.

In sunlight's glow, they shared their dreams,
Of ice cream rivers and chocolate streams.
But the wise old oak just chuckled aloud,
'You're plants, my friends, not a circus crowd.'

Yet in this patch of joy and jest,
Each leafy tale was truly the best.
For laughter blooms in the soils of cheer,
And every sprout holds a giggle near!

Dappled Tales

In the meadow, a daisy wore a hat,
While a dandelion fretted about a cat.
A buttercup whispered jokes quite sweet,
While roses strutted on their fancy feet.

A mouse once claimed to caper and dance,
But tripped on a twig—oh dear, what a chance!
The lilies laughed with petals so fine,
As the shy little violets hid from the line.

Sunflowers grinned, their faces turned bright,
Saying, 'Join us for a grand flower fight!'
They tossed around seeds, oh what a sight,
As laughter echoed into the night.

In shadows and beams, they spun their tales,
Of clumsy bees and adventurous snails.
Even the clouds giggled in delight,
As the garden whispered, 'What a fun night!'

Glimpses of Green

A tiny sprout peeked from the soil,
Said, 'Why do we toil in such a coil?'
A worm replied with a chuckling laugh,
'Just stick around for a goofy giraffe!'

The daisies protested, 'We're not for the cows!'
While clovers debated how to earn vows.
A wildflower painted with colors so bold,
Said, 'In this tale, we're never too old!'

The sunflowers posed, all glamour and grand,
While mushrooms whispered their underground band.
But the tomatoes blushed and said with a frown,
'We're just ketchup dreams turning upside down!'

As laughter erupted in the green space,
The sweet scents of joy danced all over the place.
New stories sprouted with every light breeze,
And happily shared with buzzing honeybees!

Budding Aspirations

An acorn dreamed of being a tree,
But worried it would be mighty and free.
A flower piped up, 'We'll help you grow!'
With petals of laughter and sunshine's glow.

The grass all giggled, saying, 'Join in, friend!'
'We'll grow together, there's no need to pretend.'
A playful wind tossed 'round the seeds,
Planting wishes beneath the reeds.

A wayward twig claimed to be a king,
While the carrots debated the market swing.
But all agreed that joy's the best route,
In this whimsical world, there's never a doubt!

With every bud, there blooms a cheer,
For in this garden, we find we're all near.
So let's dance in the soil, and sail on a breeze,
For life's a funny play with roots in our trees!

Growing Through the Gaps

In the cracks of the pavement, a flower popped,
It looked around, then suddenly flopped.
"What's this place?" it said with a grin,
"Do I grow here, or should I dive in?"

A weed snickered loudly, "You might be lost,
Here's where we laugh, just at any cost!
But don't feel blue, you've made a fine start,
Just wiggle your petals, and play it smart!"

The sun peeked in with a wink so bright,
"Just keep on dancing, from morning till night!
Don't worry of storms that shake you in jest,
Embrace the snickers, and you'll be blessed!"

So the flower jived in its wide-open space,
Dancing with laughter, it claimed its own place.
In the sneers and the cheers, it learned to thrive,
For growing through gaps is what keeps dreams alive!

Fleeting Flora

A petal once said, "I'm off to be grand!"
But it got stuck in a curious hand.
"Hey, let me go!" it shouted with glee,
But the child just laughed, "You're stuck here with me!"

The daisies were giggling, waving hello,
"Join us, dear petal, don't feel so low!
We dance in the breeze and share all the thrift,
It's not every day that a flower gets a lift!"

But each gust of wind took the petal away,
"Oh no! What a game! Let me choose where to sway!"
Yet up in the sky, it spun round and round,
Dancing in circles, with joy it was crowned!

So if ever you find a flower in flight,
Join in the fun, twirl with delight!
For moments are fleeting, like days full of cheer,
Enjoy every giggle, year after year!

The Harvest of Hopes

In a garden so wild, with hopes all a-sway,
Lies a pumpkin who dreamed of a grand cabaret.
"Let's gather, my friends!" it cheered with a call,
"For this harvest, we'll party, we'll dance and we'll sprawl!"

The tomatoes were blushing, the corn stood so tall,
While the carrots just chuckled, "We can't miss it all!"
With vibes so contagious, they twirled on the ground,
In the merry medley, their joy know no bounds!

As the stars twinkled down on the whimsical scene,
A scarecrow joined in, sporting pants that were green.
"Dress up for the harvest, we'll dance 'til we drop,
Just don't step on my toes, or I might just flop!"

So let's raise our glasses, filled with pumpkin pie,
And toast to the dreams that go flying on high!
For each laugh and each giggle, in the harvest we reap,
Are the tinsel of life, in our hearts they will keep!

Fertile Imaginings

In a patch full of winks, where wonder began,
A daffodil shouted, "Let's draw up a plan!
We'll trick all the critters, and scare them away,
With thoughts so wild, we'll giggle and play!"

"Who will wear what?" asked the shy little sprout,
"I'll don the bright shades that leave them in doubt!
A striped swirly hat and a careless grin,
Let's conjure up stories, let the fun begin!"

The beets soon decided to join in the fun,
Dressing up fancy, under the sun,
With shades and with hats, they all took their place,
Turning the garden into a wild space!

So if you walk by where the flowers all play,
Hear the laughter they share, join in their sway!
For in each little moment, where dreams bloom and fade,
Are fertile imaginings, in laughter we're made!

Flourishing Fables of Change

In a garden where laughter roams,
The carrots wear hats, the radishes homes.
Potatoes hold parties, with merry delight,
While beans dance around in the warm evening light.

A cabbage once claimed it was wise and so grand,
But the lettuce just chuckled, not quite what he planned.
The sunflowers giggle, swaying up high,
As the worms tell tall tales, oh my, oh my!

With each little sprout comes a tale of its own,
A radish with dreams, a zucchini alone.
They trade all their secrets, the broccoli grins,
In this wacky green world, everyone wins.

So laugh with the veggies, come join in their cheer,
For in this bright garden, true joy is sincere.
As stories take root, in the soil they'll weave,
Each one a reminder — just laugh and believe.

A Garden of Silent Confessions

In a patch where the tomatoes whisper at night,
They gossip of dreams, all bound in delight.
The carrots confess, with their roots grown so deep,
While the peas in their pods gossip over lost sleep.

The zucchini lament, they feel a bit bland,
While the herbs play it cool, so savvy and grand.
The pumpkins are plotting a Halloween scare,
As the sunflowers giggle, their royalty rare.

In this leafy abode, secrets bloom and thrive,
The potatoes are shy, but they still come alive.
The chives roll their eyes at the chattiness here,
While the kale keeps its cool, just watching with cheer.

So chalk up some laughter from plants far and wide,
For even in silence, they stand side by side.
In this nonsensical garden of jest and of glee,
There's never a dull moment for you or for me.

The Pulse of Awakening Life

When springtime arrives, with its mischievous breeze,
The flowers burst out, like they're trying to tease.
The daffodils giggle, the roses turn red,
While the tulips all twirl, spinning joy in their bed.

The bees start to buzz with a playful intent,
They tickle the blossoms, oh, to be their friend!
With petals all flapping, they join in the race,
As the daisies throw parties, each in their own space.

The grass starts to dance in the sun's warming glow,
While the clovers look on, with their giggles aglow.
The daisies wear sunglasses, so cool in their stance,
While the lilacs just sigh, "Oh, don't miss this chance!"

Life wakes up in fits, with a chuckle and grin,
A joyful parade where the laughter begins.
In this rhythmic garden, where all feel alive,
The pulse of the earth has a reason to thrive.

Hidden Stories Beneath the Soil

Underneath the dirt, where the secrets lie,
The vegetables whisper, as the worms just sigh.
The onions are sulking, their layers exposed,
While the turnips spread tales, all wrinkled and froze.

The roots intertwine, in a coat of dark plots,
As the beets share tall tales from their sweet little spots.
The hidden adventures of each hidden sprout,
Are filled with weird quirks that keep happiness stout.

The soil holds the laughter of years gone by,
With dreams of the sprouts that reach for the sky.
The carrots are crafting a novel of dreams,
With a plot twist or two that burst at the seams.

So listen real close, oh gardener dear,
For the stories below bring a chuckle and cheer.
In the laughter of roots and their quirky embrace,
Lie the hidden tales of each harvest's grace.

Nature's Open Book

Leaves turn pages in the breeze,
Every rustle brings new tease.
A squirrel pauses mid-nut bite,
Spinning tales in morning light.

Raindrops giggle on the ground,
Worms wear hats, they're quite profound.
Mushrooms dance with sprightly glee,
Whispering secrets to the bee.

Branches sway like how you feel,
Each bark has stories it can seal.
A robin sings in goofy tone,
Claiming worms as its own throne.

Nature laughs with every sigh,
As flowers bloom and birds fly high.
In this wild world, stop and look,
Every moment is a book!

The Wonder Beneath the Bark.

Underneath the roughest trunk,
Lies a kingdom of the funk.
Ladybugs wear polka dots,
Joking with the curling knots.

Beetles hold a grand parade,
Dancing shadows, they invade.
Toadstools giggle, 'What a sight!'
Amidst the chaos, pure delight.

Greenhorn shoots in quick retreat,
Trying hard to find its feet.
Meanwhile, ants strut with their load,
Thinking they're on a big road.

Beneath the bark, a world so spry,
Where shenanigans reach the sky.
Each crevice holds a silly jest,
In nature's heart, we find the best!

Whispers of the Awakening Earth

In the morning, giggles rise,
From the soil, beneath the skies.
Tiny seeds with dreams galore,
Just can't wait to explore more.

The earth hums a catchy tune,
While flowers drool at the moon.
Insects spin their web of fun,
As the day is just begun.

Grass blades tickle passing feet,
Causing stumbles and a greet.
Underneath the playful shade,
Nature jests, never afraid.

So let's join the lively throng,
Where even laughter feels so strong.
With each step, we find a cheer,
Awakening joy, year after year!

Tales of Budding Dreams

Buds pop open, tales untold,
Spinning yarns both brave and bold.
In the garden, secrets bloom,
While giggling weeds begin to loom.

A worm dons glasses, quite absurd,
Reading leaves, it sings a word.
Caterpillars throw a feast,
Where every guest is quite the beast.

The sun whispers a playful dare,
To the petals, swaying in the air.
Each breeze brings a cheeky tune,
Dancing weirdly, flowers swoon.

So gather 'round, let laughter rise,
In the world where nature sighs.
With every bloom, a story gleams,
In the land of budding dreams!

When Dreams Emerge from the Dark

In shadows where wishes do play,
A turtle dressed as a ballet.
With pirouettes and grand delight,
It dances on dreams far out of sight.

The moon chuckles with a wink,
While ants gather for a drink.
They toast with juice from wild berries,
And share the tales of great fairies.

A cat with a hat, oh so bright,
Juggles stars on a broomstick light.
He mumbles secrets of the night,
While we laugh till the morning light.

So here's to dreams that take a spin,
With laughter bubbling from within.
For in the dark where tales begin,
We find the joy of our own kin.

Threads of Green in the Fabric of Time

A sock on the line waves cheerily,
It tells of a life so merrily.
With tennis shoes dancing in stride,
They weave through time, with nowhere to hide.

The ketchup bottle dreams to be
A fancy banquet for a bee.
It plots and schemes, with great ideas,
To burst against spaghetti spheres.

Up in the clouds, a spinach leaf,
Writes letters to a wandering thief.
"Don't steal my taste!" it shouts in glee,
While plotting salad dreams, you see.

So let the greens in your pantry sing,
Of wild adventures, and delight they bring.
For in each thread of plant or vine,
A tapestry of whimsy, divine!

The Breath of Fresh Aspirations

A pickle dreams of becoming a star,
With its splashy poses, it's never afar.
The stage is set on a crusty plate,
Where cucumbers aspire to be first-rate.

Ovens giggle with bubbly cheer,
As muffins sing loud for all to hear.
With sprinkles of joy on every top,
They bounce with humor, never stop.

In gardens where radishes light the way,
They whisper secrets of bright new day.
Each leaf tickles the path of the sun,
As laughter erupts, oh what fun!

So breathe in deep, let aspirations fly,
With carrots and peas reaching high.
For each little bite of laughter we chase,
Turns meals into magic, a grand embrace!

From Tiny Seeds to Tall Legends

A seed once tiny dreamed of height,
When dandelions danced in delight.
They whispered tales of forests grand,
Of acorns plotting to take a stand.

A worm sings baritone beneath,
As old roots weave tales of its sheath.
With stories of storms and suns so bright,
The soil chuckles through the night.

The pumpkin grows with comic flair,
Donning a hat, it waves in air.
It rolls and tumbles, laughs uncontained,
As gophers cheer, all unrestrained.

So let's celebrate every sprout,
And watch the legends twist about.
For in each tiny tale we trace,
Is a giggle waiting, full of grace!

Thoughts of the Thicket

In the forest, a squirrel named Lou,
Tried to juggle acorns, just for a view.
He slipped on a branch, oh what a sight,
Fell with a thump, then laughed with delight.

A rabbit declared, 'That's quite a feat!'
As Lou righted himself with a twitch of his feet.
They danced and they leaped, oh what a show,
Forgetting their worries in the grove below.

The owl watched on with a wise little grin,
Thinking, 'What craziness, let the fun begin!'
With a wobble and bounce, they joined in the jest,
In the thicket of laughter, they felt truly blessed.

As night came to whisper a soft, silly tune,
The critters spread tales beneath the bright moon.
With giggles and grins, they tired and then dozed,
In the thicket of fun, where laughter just glows.

Radiance from the Roots

In a garden where carrots had something to say,
They hosted a party, inviting the day.
'Come join us, dear friends, with vegetables near,
We'll cook up some laughter, bring us some cheer!'

The tomatoes, quite round, rolled in with a squish,
The radishes danced, granting each veggie a wish.
Then a cucumber slipped, in the dip it did flop,
Making everyone laugh till they just couldn't stop.

The peas burst with joy, they couldn't contain,
'This garden's a riot like a wild, silly train!'
The sunflowers swayed, full of radiant glee,
Glow like a disco, oh what fun to see!

As dusk settled in, and they sang 'one last tune'
The veggies all giggled 'neath the glowing moon.
In the roots of their joy, they found something new,
Radiance of laughter, a party from stew.

The Branching Path

There once was a tree, named Grumpy McBark,
Claimed he was wise like an old, ancient shark.
But off in the branches, a parrot named Lou,
Said, 'Grumpy, my friend, we all think you stew!'

McBark rolled his eyes, with a deep, solemn laugh,
Claimed he'd give wisdom, like some mystical half.
But Lou squawked a riddle that puzzled the crowd,
'Tell me, McBark, why's your mood all so loud?'

The squirrels did chatter, chips in for a game,
With laughter and jests, they all called his name.
McBark, in the leaves, finally decided,
'Perhaps I'm just grumpy; from joy, I've divided!'

From then on the tree, he let loose a cheer,
And joined in their antics – it's silly, my dear.
The path of true fun might just twist and bend,
In the shade of each leaf, true laughter will blend.

Tales in the Taproot

In a land where the wild carrots tell jokes,
A taproot named Tim, known for clever pokes.
He whispered to herbs, with a giggle so sly,
'Hey, root friends! Let's make the veggies all cry!'

They plotted a prank, a radish disguise,
To chase down the lettuce with wide-open eyes.
But as they approached, giggles spilled out,
Radishes wheezing, they all fell about!

The tomatoes were rolling, the spinach got red,
From laughter so loud, they couldn't be fed.
But Tim, with his charm, pulled out a great tale,
Of adventures and laughter, of roots on the scale!

As twilight descended, they shared every yarn,
How the carrots once danced, all dressed in fine yarn.
In their soil, they found, with each chuckle passed down,
A taproot of joy, in their vegetable town.

Awakened Realities

In the garden of dreams, plants wear hats,
Whispering tales of mischievous cats.
They giggle and laugh, the daisies prance,
While broccoli tries its funniest dance.

The carrots joke about their roots and height,
Bantering with beans till the stars are bright.
Radishes make puns that make us snort,
As tomatoes spin tales of a veggie court.

A sunflower claims it knows the sun's song,
While peas argue if they belong to the throng.
With each silly tale, the laughter grows,
In this magical place where silliness flows.

At dusk, the veggies plot and conspire,
To start a restaurant, their one true desire.
But who will serve salads, and who's on fries?
In this world of humor, no one is wise!

Sagas in the Soil

Deep within soil, where secrets lay,
A worm tells tales of a peculiar day.
He bumped into ants in a game of chess,
Each one saying, "We're the best, we confess!"

The beetles chant in a rhythmic hum,
About the day when they stole a crumb.
Butterflies giggle, spreading their wings,
Swapping stories of peculiar things.

A snail once claimed he outran a hare,
While hedgehogs laughed, "That's quite a dare!"
Moss joins in, with a soft little grin,
Saying, "Slow and steady always wins!"

Each tale unravels in the soil's embrace,
Where laughter echoes at a funny pace.
In this earthy realm, joy's the main theme,
As life spins around like a whimsical dream.

Journal of the Wild

The forest holds tales that dance through the leaves,
Of squirrels who ponder and raccoons who tease.
A fox spins yarns about narrow escapes,
While owls give sage advice, in funny shapes.

The rabbits, though quick, often trip on their feet,
Chasing after tales of the next veggie treat.
While hedgehogs peek out, all spiky and sly,
Making wild claims about flying so high.

A deer, with a flair, attempts stand-up at night,
But knocks over mushrooms, a clumsy delight.
The laughter is loud, it fills up the trees,
In this wacky wild, it's all meant to please.

As nighttime falls, the stars wink above,
Every critter shares tales they've come to love.
In this journal of wild, the stories parade,
A fit of giggles is hilariously made.

The Blooming Chronicles

In the meadow, blooms chatter and jest,
Petals are prancing, they give it their best.
Lilies gossip about roses' bright glow,
While daisies are busy just stealing the show.

Chrysanthemums laugh about bees and their sting,
While tulips plot mischief, a curious thing.
The violets whisper, with giggles and glee,
"Telling tall tales on a bumblebee spree!"

Dandelions chuckle, their fluff in the air,
Competing for the silliest flowery flair.
As wind carries laughter from bloom to bloom,
In this garden of giggles, joy starts to zoom.

As the sun sets low, they throw a grand ball,
In hopes that the moon will join in the call.
With petals as skirts, they dance through the night,
In this blooming bliss, everything feels just right!

www.ingramcontent.com/pod-product-compliance
Lightning Source LLC
Chambersburg PA
CBHW071845160426
43209CB00003B/418